My Dog

WRITTEN BY HAYLEY NOVAK
ILLUSTRATED BY NANCY COFFELT

HARCOURT BRACE & COMPANY
Orlando Atlanta Austin Boston San Francisco Chicago Dallas New York
Toronto London

My dog can run.

My dog can jump.

My dog can walk.

My dog can bark.

My dog can nap.

My dog can sit.

My dog can hug!